Amazing, Marvelous, Wonderful Me

By Linda Pratt

Copyright © 2020 Linda Pratt,
ltg.pratt@gmail.com
ISBN 978-0-9975842-6-4

I'm just as awesome as I can be,

I'm amazing, marvelous, wonderful me!

I have eyes...

...to see the sky.

And watch the fluffy clouds float by.

I see colors, red, green, and blue.

Trees and bushes, flowers too.

And furry cats
with big blue eyes.

I watch the stars in the sky at night

And see the sun rise
big and bright.

I close my eyes to laugh and blink
Or give you a playful wink.

But what I really like to see

Are your eyes looking back at me!

of raindrops splashing on the ground.

or the zooming of a truck

I hear my sister laughing too,
when she and I play Peek-a-Boo.

And I can hear the soft tick tock

of my Grandpa's cuckoo clock.

I like to hear the buzzing bees

And birds singing in the trees,

Ringing bells,

or a beating drum

Or when you sing
or softly hum.

But what I really love to hear
Is your soft whisper in my ear.

I have a nose

to smell shampoo
And sudsy, soapy bubbles too.

I love to smell a chocolate bar
Or peanut butter in a jar.

The freshness of a woody pine
Tickles this nose of mine.

Popcorn popping fresh and hot
Is what I like to smell a lot!

And lilacs too, I like to smell those!

But best of all is sitting close side by side and nose to nose!

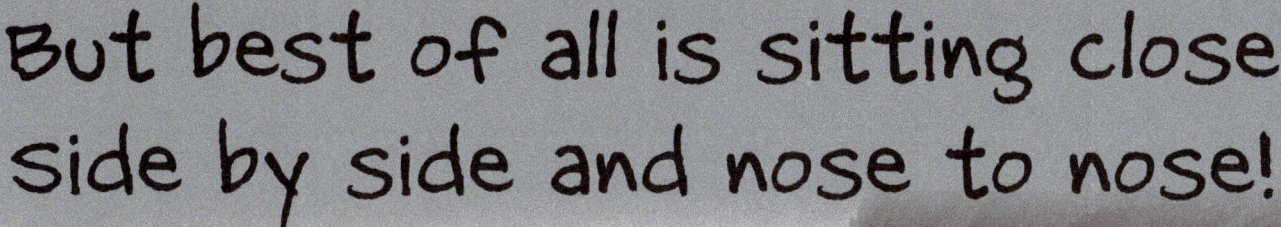

I have a mouth to smile and grin
It fits just right above my chin.

I say my name, and laugh or cry,

Or talk on the telephone.

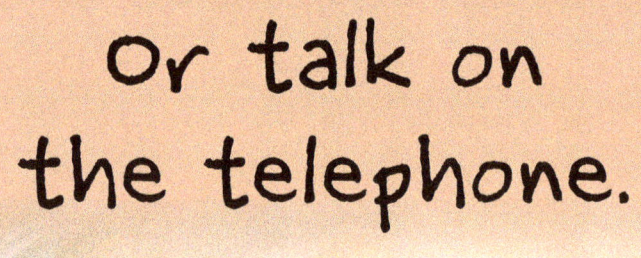

I kiss my teddy on the head,

Or taste my Grandma's gingerbread.

I have hands
to wave hello

Or make handprints
in the snow.

I can help my Daddy cook,

Or turn the pages of a book.

I dig in my garden,
then plant some seeds.

Water them and pull
the weeds.

I count my fingers,
one by one,

Then clap my hands
when I am done.

I put on my own shoes and socks,

And build a tower with my blocks.

After my hands are done with play

I slip them into yours each day.

I have feet to play outside

To walk and skip, to climb and slide.

Then step up on my special stool.

And dance to happy music too.

I kick through scattered Autumn leaves That have fallen from the trees.

I wiggle my toes on the bathroom rug

After we pull the bathtub plug.

Then, every night when day is through, I use my feet to run to you.

I'm just as awesome
as I can be,

I'm amazing, marvelous,
wonderful me!

Think of all the amazing, marvelous, and wonderful things you can do! How do you like to use your eyes, ears, nose, mouth, hands and feet? Don't wait to start using your senses and abilities to explore the world around you! Now is the time to try something new!

www.ingramcontent.com/pod-product-compliance
Lightning Source LLC
Chambersburg PA
CBHW040001290426
43673CB00077B/294